THE OLD MINERAL LINE

R. J. Sellick

HALSGROVE

First published in Great Britain 1976
Second Revised edition 1981 Reprinted 1988, 1996, 2003, 2007
Third Revised edition 2012

Copyright © R.J. Sellick

Cover image: *Comberow and the Incline* H. H. Hole (see also p.23)

British Library Cataloguing-in-Publication Data

A CIP record for this title is available from the British Library

ISBN 978 0 85704 188 3

HALSGROVE
Halsgrove House
Ryelands Business Park
Bagley Road, Wellington
Somerset TA21 9PZ
T: 01823 653777
F: 01823 216796
email: sales@halsgrove.com
website: www.halsgrove.com

Printed and bound by
HSW Print Ltd, Tonypandy

Contents

Exploring

Most of the line is now privately owned; and so anyone wishing to visit places, which are on private property, should seek permission first.

The Author

After attending the tiny village school at Herner, in the Taw Valley, R. J. Sellick went to Barnstaple Grammar School and later to Taunton School. A Chartered Surveyor, his work took him all over the country, from Plymouth to Sheffield, but latterly his permanent home was at Luxborough, only three miles from the West Somerset Mineral Railway.

His interest in the mineral line dated from his schoolboy days when, his curiosity aroused by his father's stories of the derelict line, he explored the route by cycle and on foot and interviewed many who had worked on or remembered the railway and mines. Much later, in 1962, he wrote *The West Somerset Mineral Railway*, the standard history on the subject, which has since been re-issued in a second edition. He also compiled a new extended edition of C. S. Orwin's classic history. *The Reclamation of Exmoor Forest* and edited E. T. MacDermot's notes for the new edition of *The History of the Forest of Exmoor*, all published by David & Charles of Newton Abbot.

Author's Acknowledgements

The diagram map of the WSMR, inside the front cover, is by Robert Winn.

Many of the photographs reproduced are by H. H. Hole, or come from the Hole collection, by courtesy of Victor Bonham-Carter, while those in the LGRP collection are included by kind permission of David & Charles of Newton Abbot, proprietors of Locomotive and General Railway Photographs. Unless otherwise attributed the remaining illustrations were taken by me, or are from my collection; and I should like to express my thanks to my co-authors in the history of the West Somerset Mineral Railway, John Hamilton and Michael Jones, and to A. L. Wedlake, author of *A History of Watchet*, for making photographs available to me.

R.J.S.

Chapter One

The West Somerset Mineral Railway

History

An independent and sometimes eccentric line, which connected the local port of Watchet with long abandoned mines and deserted villages more than 1,000 feet high on the Brendon Hills, the WSMR enjoys a place in West Somerset folklore unrivalled by any closed branch line. Rarely accorded its full title, it is invariably referred to with nostalgic affection as 'the old mineral line', and indeed this has become an official address both at Watchet and Roadwater. Its history, too, is of much greater interest than one would normally expect of a mineral railway about twelve miles long.

There had been sporadic mining for iron ore on the Brendon Hills since at least Elizabethan, and possibly Roman, times, but extensive working did not take place until the partners of the Ebbw Vale iron-works formed the Brendon Hills Iron Ore Company in 1853. The following year they promoted the West Somerset Mineral Railway to carry the iron ore to Watchet on the Bristol Channel, whence it would be shipped to Newport and on to Ebbw Vale. An Act of Parliament was obtained in 1855 for a 4 ft. 8.5 in. gauge line from Watchet to the principal mine at Raleigh's Cross, and thence to continue to Heath Poult at the western end of the Brendons.

Work on the line started in May 1856, but although a first locomotive arrived that November it was put out of action after only two months when the stoker forgot to fill the boiler before lighting the fire. However by April 1857 the railway was open from Watchet to Roadwater, which served as a temporary railhead for ore from the mines, but that August a more serious accident occured when the two engines which were then working the line collided head on at Kentsford, killing three men. Despite this the line reached Comberow, at the foot of the hills, by December, but to reach the summit, 800 feet above, a gigantic incline had to be built, three quarters of a mile long at a gradient of 1 in 4. To dispose of the mounting stocks of ore at the mines this incline was opened with makeshift machinery on 31 May 1858, but it was not until March 1861 that it was finally finished, the line having in the meantime been leased to the BHIOCo for seven years from 1859.

Considerable difficulty had been experienced at Watchet harbour where the pier was unusable and carts had to be driven alongside the beached vessels at low water. After litigation and a public enquiry, the Watchet Harbour Act 1857 placed it under the control of commissioners who constructed a new east pier and rebuilt the west pier with a break-water extension, the work being completed in 1862. That year also marked the opening of the broad gauge West Somerset Railway from Norton Fitzwarren (on the Bristol & Exeter Railway). The WSR had unsuccessfully sought running powers over the WSMR, which would have been converted to mixed gauge, but in fact there was never a connection between them, the broad gauge using the east pier and the narrow gauge the west, even after the former was extended to Minehead in 1874.

The completed section of the WSMR to the Raleigh's Cross mine had cost over £82,000 (against an estimate of £65,000 for the whole railway) and in consequence it was not until 1863 that work started on the western extension. This was opened to Gupworthy by September 1864, but no work was ever undertaken between there and Heath Poult. A new lease of the whole line was granted that year direct to the Ebbw Vale Company Ltd. (which had also taken over the mines) to terminate in September 1919, and as before the mining company was to provide locomotives and rolling stock and operate the line.

By now there were extensive mining operations from Colton in the east to Eisen Hill nine miles to the west, and small mining villages had grown up around the Raleigh's Cross and Gupworthy mines with cottages, a shop, chapels, and two mission churches also used as schools. To serve these isolated communities a public passenger service from Watchet to Comberow was started on 4 September 1865, and it was possible to travel up the incline and on to Gupworthy in a truck, free, but at one's own risk. The railway now settled down to a busy, if placid existence, marred only by a startling accident in December 1876, when three timber waggons ran back down the line from Roadwater, pursued by a frantically whistling locomotive, and ultimately came to rest on Watchet pier. Another 'runaway' took place in November 1882, when a derailed locomotive and two coal waggons bumped over the sleepers half way down the incline.

A recession in the iron and steel trade, coupled with competition from Spanish ore, caused the mines to close in May 1879, and although some were reopened the following November, a final closure took place in September 1883, and the railway passenger service was in consequence reduced to two mixed trains daily. This lasted until 7 November 1898, when all traffic ceased, and the rolling stock was removed to Ebbw Vale by means of a temporary connection to the GWR Minehead branch at Kentsford.

In 1907 the Somerset Mineral Syndicate was formed to work the iron ore and lease the railway. The Syndicate bought various waggons and a cheap, but entirely unsuitable, former Metropolitan Railway engine, which it used as far as Comberow, and also reopened the incline but not the line from there to Gupworthy. No passenger service was run, but to celebrate the reopening a public excursion was arranged to Comberow on 4 July, complete with Watchet Council and the town band. Only two mines were worked, at Timwood (near Comberow) and at Colton, to which a two-mile long steam-worked two-foot gauge tramway was laid from the top of the incline. Unfortunately the venture collapsed in March 1910, the equipment (including the locomotive and waggons) being sold by auction on 28 June.

The line was not quite dead, for an Australian inventor, A. R. Angus, took over the section between Watchet and Washford in December 1911 to demonstrate a system of automatic train control he had patented. Two ex-GWR locomotives were used, and at a public demonstration on 5 July 1912 these were sent off driverless from opposite ends of the line, pulling up automatically some 200 yards apart, much to the disappointment of some of the crowd who had hoped to see a head-on collision. With the wartime steel shortage the Ministry of Munitions commandeered the rails as scrap in 1917, and although they were not all removed until the end of the war, by 1919 the line was without rails or rolling stock. An Act of Parliament was therefore obtained to abandon the line, and the land and buildings were sold by auction on 8 August 1924, the company finally being wound up the following year.

The full story of the railway and the mines and mining communities which it served, is told in R.J.Sellick's book *The West Somerset Mineral Railway* (published by David & Charles) from which these brief details are taken. Readers are also recommended to seek out *The Brendon Hills Iron Mines and the West Somerset Mineral Railway* by M. H. Jones (Lightmoor Press, 2011), which incorporates the results of much new research and archaeological investigation and is now the standard modern work on the subject.

Exploring the line

Many WSMR sites are accessible on foot by following public rights of way. A good map is essential and Ordnance Survey map OL9 covers Exmoor National Park and includes the Brendon Hills and Watchet. A series of leaflets about the railway and giving detailed information about the accessible sites is available from National Park Centres, local Tourist Information centres, Raleigh's Cross Inn, and Watchet Market House Museum. Most of the line is now privately owned and, with the increasing number of visitors, the thoughtless few who leave gates open and damage fences have forced owners to be less tolerant of trespassing. The following notes show how to see what is left of the railway from routes open to the public, but anyone particularly wishing to visit places which are on private property should seek permission first – it is seldom refused.

Today Watchet harbour's once busy trade in general merchandise has given way to leisure use and a picturesque Marina. There is an interpretation board on the west pier, which was used by the WSMR and still shows traces of the rails. It is open to the public and reached through an archway beside the London Inn in Market Street. The railway crossed Market Street on the level to reach the station, and the two-storey station house and offices, the wooden goods shed (now a restaurant) and the stone goods shed beyond it can be seen from the road. The line can be rejoined by taking the footpath to the east of Station House (by the Star Inn) which leads to Whitehall, where a row of houses stands on the site of the former engine shed. From here the mineral line is a public footpath which runs under the West Somerset Railway and then parallel to it past Kentsford until, approaching Washford, the right-of-way diverges to the right through a playing field, avoiding a private house which has been built on the track.

A modern bungalow stands on the site of Washford station, which was between Lower Washford level crossing and the bridge carrying the main Williton to Minehead road over the line. A good view of the track can be seen from this road and although there is no path to the south, by taking the road up the valley by Cleeve Abbey (which is well worth visiting) the railway can be seen again at Torre level crossing. Here there is still the crossing keeper's hut dated 1871 and, looking back towards Washford, a cutting through the new red sandstone which was quarried here to provide stone for many of the buildings and bridges on the line. Above Torre crossing, part of the track has been obliterated by tipping. There is no path, but the route can be seen from the valley road rejoining the line at Clitsome, where the gatekeeper's hut and one pair of the level crossing gates still survive.

From Clitsome to Roadwater station the railway has been largely taken into adjoining properties and in places built over, but the abutments of one of the bridges over the Washford River can be seen from the road, as can a section of the track as it runs through the recreation ground on a slight embankment. The entrance to Roadwater station yard was by the bridge in the centre of the village and part of the original wooden goods shed remains, as well as the station building which has been skilfully converted to a private bungalow. A good view of the station and of a river bridge (with the original girders still in position) can be seen from the level crossing, which is reached by taking the narrow lane on the left just after the station entrance.

The next mile and a half of the railway has been made into a public road to serve the hamlets of Higher and Lower Hayne, and where this ends at Pit Mill an unmade track continues along the line to Comberow, which is open to the public as a footpath. Scenically this is the finest section of the line, for Combe Row (as it is pronounced and was often spelt) signifies the head of the valley and there are lofty wooded hills on three sides, with the incline ascending the steep slope of one of them. The station itself has long been demolished for its stone, but the station-master's house, rebuilt after a fire, is much as it ever was, and there is a fine stone arch under the foot of the incline.

In 1998 the Exmoor National Park Authority purchased the track bed of the incline and it was scheduled as an Ancient Monument. They have installed iron steps at the foot of the incline as part of permitted access there so you can get up onto the incline from the bottom. The difficulties of building this immense incline are vividly illustrated by the rock cuttings which still show the drill holes made for blasting, and at the half-way point there is a fine waterfall where a stream is carried under the line to emerge high above the ravine below. There is now permitted access from the top of the incline eastwards to the rights of way network. If you would rather, shortly before the incline runs out of the woods it is crossed by a way-marked walk, and the left-hand path provides a convenient way of reaching the road along the crest of the Brendons. Alternatively the right-hand path makes a most attractive walk back to Comberow, passing a waterslide at one point.

The upper path joins the top road midway between the Raleigh's Cross Hotel and Brendon Hill, and going westward along the road the first place of interest is Beulah, a Methodist chapel built for the mining community in 1861. By taking the Bampton road for a quarter of a mile the foundations of the once extensive Raleigh's Cross mine can be seen on the left (this also was robbed for its stone), and soon after the railway goods yard with its ruined stores is on the right. Returning to Beulah and turning sharp left on to the Wheddon Cross road the ruins of a row of miner's dwellings, Beulah Cottages, are on the right, followed by the still impressive Mines Captain's residence, Sea View House. Here at the top of the incline the railway emerged on to a great embankment, crossed the road and ran through Brendon Hill station to reach the goods yard and turn west along the ridge of the hills. The station (now a bungalow) is private, as is the farmhouse beside it, which was once the general stores serving the mining village. The Winding House at the top of the incline contained winding drums which lowered waggons of iron ore down the slope and hauled empty waggons back up. In 2009 a Heritage Lottery grant allowed the conservation of the Winding House. From the embankment by the Winding House on a clear day the view is so extensive that it might have been said that the steelworks at Ebbw Vale could be seen from the mines at Brendon Hill.

All of the railway remains to the south of the Wheddon Cross B3224 road lie on private land. From Brendon Hill to Gupworthy the railway, though clearly defined, has been incorporated into neighbouring farms and there is no path along it. The best way to see what is left is to use the Wheddon Cross road as a base line, and make short diversions along the various roads running from it to the south. The first of these leaves the main road at Sminhays Cottages, the only terrace of miners' cottages still occupied, and leads to Naked Boy's Bridge. This is named after the nearby Naked Boy's stone but, like almost all the bridges crossing public roads, was demolished when the railway was abandoned, to avoid future maintenance. There is permitted access west from the bridge near Naked Boy's stone along the trackbed of the line to connect with the right of way that runs roughly north-south across that area. A third of a mile west of Sminhays Cottages a distant view of the ruined engine house at Burrow Farm mine can be seen from the main road. The Exmoor National Park Authority conserved the remains of the Burrow Farm Engine House in 1990 and although it is on privately-owned land there is a permitted footpath to the site (not accessible in April, and no dogs at any time). By taking the next fork left the railway can be crossed at Eastcott Bridge and again at Withiel Bridge.

The line now runs on an embankment (parallel to the ridge road) at the far end of which only a few stones remain to mark the site of Luxborough Road station, and there is also little to show the route of the branch which soon after crossed the road to reach Langham Hill mine to the north. The conserved remains of Langham Hill Engine House and Bearland Wood Ventilation Flue lie in the Forestry Commission's Chargot Woods, and can be accessed by public trails from the car park on the north side of the B3224. The next road to the south is Blagdon lane which leads to Gupworthy Bridge, while 350 yards further west is an unmade track which served Gupworthy mine. Here the railway ran through the mine yard, with the drift, engine house and mining hamlet on its north side, and the spoil tip to the south. A pair of miners' cottages was converted into a chapel in which regular services were held until 1972, but this has since been engulfed by a new bungalow, which has the drift in the garden and an outbuilding that was once the mine drying shed.

Beyond Gupworthy mine a branch railway forked south to Gupworthy New Pit while the main line curved north west to its terminus. This is reached by returning to the Wheddon Cross road and then taking the next turning to the south, Armoor lane, (sign-posted Brompton Regis), from which there is an excellent view of the station from the buffer stops adjoining the road. The station house is still occupied and some of the buildings remain, so that it is not difficult to visualise how it used to look. Some 550 yards to the north, at Kennesome Hill mine, was the other long surviving engine house, but after having stood derelict for 95 years it was blown up by the Forestry Commission in 1978 as being unsafe.

Chapter Two
The Photographers

Regrettably little is known about the pioneer photographer who was responsible for many of the earliest illustrations, James Date. A Watchet man, he lived at Myrtle House in Swain Street, and may well have been the 'draper and grocer' of that name listed in an 1840 directory. His interest in photography probably started as an amateur, but at some time between 1861 and 1866 he set up in business as a 'photographic artist', which he combined with letting apartments. Although in 1877 the photographic business was sold, he was still letting lodgings until his death in 1895 at the age of 88.

James Date's main source of income would have been from portraits, but he also took a large number of views, often using a stereoscopic camera, mainly in West Somerset and North Devon but including some taken on a visit to France in 1871. Few of Date's negatives still survive, but by good fortune he made an album of his work for his grand daughter who bequeathed it to her niece, Mrs. P. O. Lyddon of Minehead, and with her kind permission copies of many of his photographs have been made.

In contrast the firm of Herbert H. Hole of Williton closed only in 1974. Herbert Henry Hole had set up in business in Long Street originally as a printer, bookbinder and stationer in 1856 at the age of 21. two years later he took up photography with such success that he was able to give up printing and bookbinding work. Initially he took mainly portraits but by the last decade of the 19th century was taking some very fine views, using whole plate and larger glass negatives. The venture flourished and in 1877 he acquired James Date's business, soon after opening a branch at Minehead in Friday Street. Fortunately he retained a few of Date's negatives and it is thanks to this that they survive today, even though the Watchet business was subsequently closed.

When Herbert Hole died in 1900 the Minehead branch, now in The Avenue, was being run by his son Frank, while the Williton studio was continued at first by Mrs. Hole. On his return from training in London in 1903 it was taken over by the youngest son, Walter, who with his brother built up a considerable trade in local view post-cards. Following Frank's death in 1911 the Minehead branch was closed within a year or two, but Walter continued the main business at Williton until his own death in 1946.

The firm now passed to the third generation, Herbert Henry like his grandfather, who continued the business until his retirement in 1974, and to whom I am indebted for many of these notes. He added to the family collection of West Somerset Mineral Railway photographs by copying a number of James Date's prints for which negatives no longer existed. When he retired, all the historic negatives were sold to Victor Bonham-Carter and Michael Bouquet.

Whereas the Williton and Minehead studios of H. H. Hole were run as two branches of the family firm, the business of Bert Hole was entirely separate. Herbert Hole had married twice and Bert Hole, his son by his first marriage, had set up on his own account in Swain Street, Watchet, some time between 1894 and 1897. Competition between the two firms was keen and both issued sets of postcards showing the reopening of the railway and mines, though the majority were taken by Bert Hole since he not only rather specialised in topical postcards, but the fortunes of Watchet were more closely bound up with the mining venture than those of Williton or Minehead. Bert Hole continued as a general and portrait photographer at least until 1935, but after his death his widow remained in business only as a tobacconist.

Daniel Nethercott was a Roadwater photographer who was born about 1829, the fourth child of a local farmer. He first became a stone mason, but in his thirties trained as a photographer, reputedly in London where one of his brothers lived. One of his surviving negatives is a view of St. Paul's from the river. On his return he built a darkroom and studio at the family farm at Druids Combe where he undertook whatever work was offered: portraits of local people, pictures of their houses, even 'Mr. Risdon's Prize Bull'. He recorded anything that interested him, from a local election to a visit by the Church Army, as well as the mineral railway both before 1898 and after 1907, but since photography alone did not provide a living, Daniel Nethercott continued to work locally as a mason. Although a number of his negatives survived his death in 1918 many were subsequently damaged by damp, and the few still in existence were either kindly given by Miss Date of Beggearn Huish to the author or are owned by Dr. Glyn Court of Washford.

While the earlier photographs were the work of professionals, almost all the later ones were taken by amateurs. A. W. Bartlett, a member of The Railway Club, visited the line in 1908 and again in 1911, while T. R. Perkins, a chemist from Henley-in-Arden well known for his interest in railway byeways, photographed the abandoned route in 1933. W. E. Hayward was no photographer, though his results were surprisingly good considering that they were taken with his wife's camera wrapped in a handkerchief to keep it lightproof! He was primarily a collector of railway history material, including photographs and relics, being particularly interested in the Lynton and Barnstaple Railway and the WSMR. Always delighted to help others during his lifetime, at his death he bequeathed 776 files of his collection to British Transport Historical Records.

Chapter Three

The Nineteenth Century

The mineral line until its closure in 1898

High tide at Watchet about 1890. A steamship unloads its cargo at the east pier, while in the background sailing craft lie alongside the mineral railway jetty at the west pier, no longer used for shipping iron ore. (*H. H. Hole*).

Broad gauge on the east pier at Watchet, about 1872. This was served by the West Somerset Railway from the main Bristol and Exeter line at Norton Fitzwarren, whereas the west pier and mineral jetty in the background were narrow gauge worked by the WSMR. *(James Date).*

It was in sailing craft such as these that the iron ore was conveyed to Newport on its way to the steelworks at Ebbw Vale. Behind them on the mineral jetty are the hydraulic tippers installed in 1874 to discharge complete waggon loads of ore direct into the ships' holds. *(James Date).*

Watchet station looking north towards the harbour, about 1875. The tall building at the far end of the platform by the level crossing gates housed the railway company's offices. (*James Date, A. L. Wedlake collection*).

Pontypool on the afternoon mixed train at Watchet about 1875. The horse was used to pull the waggons between the station and the mineral jetty. (*James Date*).

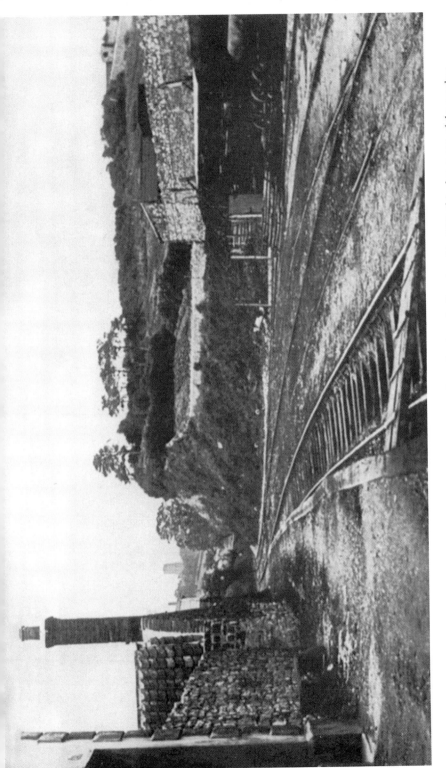

Watchet station yard looking south towards the Brendons. Taken about the time the line closed in 1898, this shows one of the coaches relegated to use as a store. (*LGRP collection*).

Roadwater village in the 1890s with the Brendon Hills as a backcloth. The station yard can clearly be seen even though the platform is hidden behind the trees. *(Daniel Nethercott).*

Comberow station, looking towards Watchet. Taken soon after the opening of the line to passengers in 1865, this view shows the locomotive *Rowcliffe*, which worked the lower section alone from 1857 until the arrival of *Pontypool* in 1866. *(James Date)*.

Comberow from the hill, about 1875. In the foreground is the stationmaster's house, and behind it the passenger coaches wait at the platform while *Pontypool* shunts the waggons for the afternoon mixed train to Watchet. *(James Date)*.

The foot of the incline showing a waggon descending, about 1875. The crude semaphore signal was controlled from the winding house and lowered to give warning that winding was about to start. . *(Robert Gillo).*

A companion photograph of the incline, taken from above the Comberow farm underbridge about 1875. Except for the lowest few yards, where it ran on rollers, the cable was guided by sheaves, one of which can be seen between the rails, which on the incline were spiked direct to the sleepers and not chaired as elsewhere on the line. The wires controlled the semaphore signals at the top and bottom of the incline, while the disc and crossbar signal protected the station. (*James Date*).

The immense size of the incline is shown dramatically in this photograph taken in 1895. (*H. H. Hole*).

Comberow and the incline. On a summer morning in 1895 *Pontypool* waits with the
10.45a.m. train to Watchet. *(H. H. Hole).*

Secured to the incline cable by triple chains, th waggon was used by passengers who travelle free at their own risk. By the 1890s the line was s run down that the incline signal semaphore ar had fallen off, and for some time the only warnin was given by the counterweight. *(W. E. Hayway collection).*

The 'Iron Church' and incline top at Brendon Hill about 1870. This mission hall was also used as a schoo during the week. Behind it is the incline brakesman's hut and the railway embankment leading to th bridge over the Wheddon Cross road. *(Daniel Nethercott).*

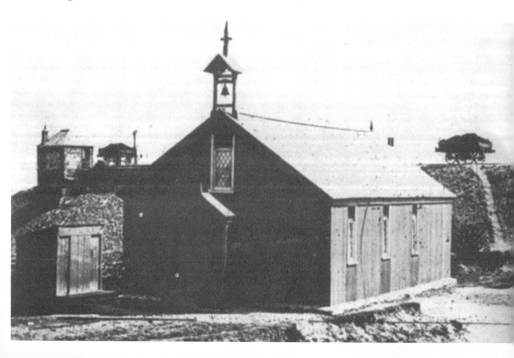

Langham Hill mine about 1870. The branch from Luxborough Road station can be seen as it enters the mine yard by the engine house, while in the foreground is the aerial rope-way from Kennesome Hill mine. *(James Date).*

Inside the winding house. In the photograph opposite, which dates from the same period, the winding house is hidden behind the Iron Church, but this interior view shows the massive size of the 18-ft. cable drums, dwarfing the engineer, Jim Hoyles. *(J. Hamilton collection).*

The 'Box' engine at the top of the incline about 1890, driven by Tom Stevens with his son Charlie as fireman This locomotive had been delivered new from Neilson of Glasgow in 1856, but latterly was normally used only on the top section of the line *(H. H. Hole)*.

This photograph of the 'Box' and its crew was taken at Gupworthy also about 1890. As on the incline, the passengers on the first truck had travelled free but at their own risk. *(J. Hamilton collection)*.

Pontypool, photographed at Watchet shed after having been rebuilt in 1895. The crew is (from left to right), Joe Duddridge (guard), Nicholas Redd (driver) and James Wood (fireman) with his small son Edmund. *(H. H, Hole).*

While *Pontypool* was being fitted with vacuum brakes in 1894, the line was worked by another Sharp Stewart engine, *Esperanza*, also photographed at Watchet shed. *(W. E. Hayward collection).*

The official maker's photograph of *Pontypool* taken in 1866 at Sharp Stewart's Manchester works shortly before delivery to the WSMR. *(J. Mudd. North British Locomotive Co. collection).*

Chapter Four

Closed to Traffic

The mineral line between 1898 and 1917 (except for the periods when it was worked by the Somerset Mineral Syndicate and A. R. Angus).

The empty engine shed, overgrown track and leaning signal epitomise the disused railway. This photograph of Whitehall and the approach to Watchet station was taken in May 1911. *(A. W. Bartlett, LGRP collection).*

Watchet harbour after the great storm of 28-29 December 1900. The east and west piers and the mineral jetty still stand, but a great breach was made in the wooden breakwater. *(Courtesy Mrs. Strong, Watchet).*

Rebuilding the harbour, 1904. The 'mineral yard' by the west pier was used as a depot, and in the background the station goods sheds can be seen.

A forlorn picture of Washford in May 1911 after the departure of the Mineral Syndicate and the removal of its rolling stock and equipment. *(A. W. Bartlett)*.

A pig roots among the rusting rails at Comberow in May 1911, though the booking office still contained its ticket rack and dating press. *(A. W. Bartlett, LGRP collection)*.

A bleak view of Brendon Hill lying derelict about 1905. The engine house water tower dominates the foreground, and behind it are Davis's Stores, the station, and on the extreme right the chimney to Carnarvon mine engine house. *(H. H. Hole).*

A companion photograph from the Wheddon Cross road showing railway arch and the incline winding house. *(H. H. Hole).*

In May 1911 Brendon Hill station was again uninhabited and shuttered after its brief re-opening. In the background is the engine house, water tower and the brakesman's hut at the top of the incline, and on the right Davis's Stores. *(A. W. Bartlett, LGRP collection).*

Stripped of all removable fittings when the mines closed in 1883, this is all that remained of the once impressive pumping and winding houses at Raleigh's Cross mine by 1905. Soon nothing would remain, for the Mineral Syndicate quarried what was left to counterbalance loads of stores coming up the incline in 1907. *(H. H. Hole).*

LEIGH'S CROSS MINE, BRENDON HILL.

OLD CHAPEL, BRENDON HILL.

When Beulah Chapel was opened on 31 May 1861 'the parties connected with the iron mines were thanked for their interest and help', but when the mines closed the congregation disappeared. By 1890 the 'blistering walls, boarded windows and overthrown railings' were 'a sad commentary on its title', but fifteen years later there were no windows to board. *(H. H. Hole)*.

When the mines were in full work the miners drank and often fought at the Raleigh's Cross Inn. More peaceable in 1905 it continued to serve the rural community, being famous for its autumn sheep auctions, which still take place in the adjoining field today. *(H. H. Hole)*.

RALEIGH'S CROSS HOTEL, BRENDON HILL

Even though closed to traffic the mineral line was supposed to be maintained in working order. This old gentleman, photographed in Smith's cutting on Withiel Hill in May 1911, lived at Gupworthy station and had the task of looking after the entire upper section. *(A. W. Bartlett, LGRP collection).*

Luxborough Road station had been built in anticipation of a passenger service to Gupworthy which did not materialise. In 1893 it was 'much dilapidated and of no use whatever' and by May 1911 it was a ruin. *(A. W. Bartlett, LGRP collection).*

Gupworthy bridge in May 1911, looking east. Like all the bridges on the upper section, this was demolished when the line was abandoned in 1923. (*A. W. Bartlett, LGRP collection*).

Apart from the rails, Gupworthy terminus could have easily been mistaken for a farm when this was taken about 1908. As the Mineral Syndicate had no mines in the vicinity, it did not reopen the line beyond Brendon Hill. (*LGRP collection*).

Chapter Five
Reopenings

The Somerset Mineral Syndicate 1907-1910
The Angus brake trials 1912

After a lapse of 25 years Watchet once again heard the roar
of iron ore being tipped into a ship's hold when the first out-
put of the Mineral Syndicate was despatched aboard the
Lizzie on 4 February 1908. The mineral jetty had been
removed during the harbour rebuilding, and this same
length of the west pier had been used to unload the
Syndicate's first waggons from the *Mary Louisa* eight months
earlier. *(Bert Hole).*

The Syndicate's locomotive, former Metropolitan Railway No. 37, was hauled dead by rail over the GWR to Kentsford where a temporary connection was made between the Minehead branch and the WSMR. The transfer took place on Sunday 30 June 1907 and the top photograph shows the arrival of No. 37 behind a GWR engineer's train. It was then uncoupled and is seen in the lower illustration as it ran back by gravity on to the WSMR and thence to Watchet. *(Bert Hole).*

Steam was raised for the first time on 3 July 1907 when the engine and one truck ventured as far as Roadwater. The upper picture shows it running into Washford station while at Roadwater most of the village pose in front of the train in the lower photograph. *(Bert Hole)*.

To celebrate the reopening of the line a public excursion was run on 4 July 1907, but its departure was delayed by a torrential hailstorm. Here the engine and its four truck loads of somewhat dampened passengers, including Watchet council members and the town band, are about to leave Watchet. (Bert Hole)

By the time the excursion reached Comberow the sun had come out and the train and its passengers were photographed again, with the town band well to the fore. *(Bert Hole)*.

The last reopening celebration took place on 17 July 1907 when the first truck was hauled to the top of the incline. The stationary engine not being available, teams of horses had to pull a laden platelayers' trolley down the gradient to act as a counterweight for the ascending truck. Here flags blow in the breeze above the winding house at Brendon Hill during the day long operation. *(Bert Hole)*.

In sad contrast to the earlier enthusiasm, by the time this photograph of Watchet station yard was taken in August 1909 the Syndicate was in difficulties and the line little used. (*Locomotive Publishing Company*).

This picture of the maintenance gang and their trolley was taken near Bye Farm above Kentsford about 1912 and shows Billy Willis (in white coat and broad brimmed hat) with Jim Vickery holding the hand crank and the foreman Mr. Hodge on the right. *(J. Hamilton collection).*

Washford station can be seen beyond the ore briquetting plant the Mineral Syndicate built there in 1909, while in the foreground is the Robey stationary engine removed from the incline winding house. *(H. H. Hole).*

Roadwater station, seen here in 1908 with its caretaker Mr. Howe, was of the same neat design as Washford, Comberow and Brendon Hill. *(A. W. Bartlett, LGRP collection).*

When this photograph at Comberow was taken in 1908 the Metropolitan Railway badge had been painted out, the numerals taken off the chimney and the condensing gear removed from the locomotive. This was much too heavy for the line and nearly jumped the track at one bend on its return to Roadwater. *(A. W. Bartlett).*

mwood Tunnel was the only new
ine opened by the Mineral Syndi-
te and it was driven into the foot
the Brendons with the intention of
tersecting the iron lodes at depth,
t money ran out before ore bear-
g ground was reached. The miner
the centre is carrying explosives
r rock blasting. *(H. H. Hole).*

To reach a loading bank the mine tramway from Timwood Tunnel crossed the
mineral railway by a moveable crossing about a quarter mile north of Comberow.
The compressor house and mine buildings were barely complete when this photograph was taken in the winter of 1907-8. *(Bert Hole).*

Comberow from the incline in 1908. The former Metropolitan Railway locomotive is
taking water while at the side of the incline the original semaphore signalling system
has been supplemented by a telephone line which ran from Brendon Hill to Watchet.
(Bert Hole LGRP collection).

The reopening of the mines provided extra trade to The Stores at Brendon Hill, and this lively picture is in great contrast to that on page 32, as both miners and local families come to do their weekend shopping. *(Bert Hole).*

Brendon Hill station was used as the Syndicate's offices and their employees were photographed here one Saturday pay day in 1908. *(Bert Hole).*

To reach the reopened Colton mine the Syndicate laid a two-foot gauge light railway from Brendon Hill alongside the main road past Raleigh's Cross, and thence down an incline into Galloping Bottom. In the top photograph the Kerr Stuart locomotive and its diminutive train crosses the road opposite the Raleigh's Cross Inn on its way to Brendon Hill, while in the lower picture the Bagnall engine is about to leave Colton incline top. (*Above – Bert Hole. Below – H. H. Hole, J. Hamilton collection*).

The incline was laid down the slope of the hill at varying gradients, and as there were no compensating loads the waggons of iron ore had to be hauled to the summit with the assistance of a winding engine. The winding house can be seen here at the incline top and also in the background in the preceding photograph *(opposite below). (Bert Hole).*

To take this picture inside Colton mine the photographer used magnesium flash powder. In the iron mines, unlike collieries, there was no risk of explosion from fire damp, and candle lanterns were used for lighting. *(H. H. Hole).*

On 5 July 1912 there was a public demonstration of the Angus automatic train control system on the mineral line between Watchet and Washford. Above, former GWR locomotive 212, decorated with the Australian flag, waits by the engine shed at Whitehall, Watchet. The wooden extension had been specially added to accommodate the two tender engines.

Below, sister locomotive 213 passes Kentsford crossing on one of the test runs.   (*Above – LGRP collection. Below – Bert Hole*).

Chapter Six
Abandoned

The mineral line since the track was lifted in 1917.

The old railway trackbed still serving a useful purpose as a track for road vehicles. Since this wintry scene was taken near Pit Farm in 1962, the line has become a surfaced public road from Roadwater as far as Pit Mill.

This view of Watchet harbour taken about 1950 makes an interesting contrast with that on page 14 taken some 60 years earlier. The mineral jetty has gone and the wooden breakwater has been replaced with a solid stone structure after the storm damage at the beginning of the century. (*H. H. Hole*).

52

Once a familiar sight this 1951 photograph shows a train leaving the east pier laden with esparto grass from the S.S. *Margol*. This and wood pulp were imported for the Watchet paper mills and others elsewhere in the West Country. Apart from the gauge the method of transhipment is the same as the 1872 view on page 15.

In this mid-twentieth-century view, the mineral railway station at Watchet is now a garage but the stone goods shed on the left, the wooden goods shed in the centre and the station house on the right still remain, though the platform was enclosed to make a skittle alley. It is still recognisable as the station in the 19th century photographs on page 16, and in those in 1907 and 1909 on pages 40 and 42.

In this evening photograph from Cleeve Hill above Watchet only hedgerows mark the mineral line as it curves south towards the Brendons, parallel with Great Western Minehead branch. It was from this vantage point that spectators witnessed the Angus trials in 1912 shown on page 50.

Though nothing remains of Washford station, a mile to the south Torre level crossing is still recognisable the same today as in this 1938 photograph. To the north of the crossing, beyond the gatekeeper's hut with its 1871 datestone, is the quarry which supplied building stone for many of the stations and bridges *(W. E. Hayward).*

The next crossing up the line was at Clitsome, Lower Roadwater, shown here in 1938 looking north. Since then the gatekeeper's hut has been repaired to make a summerhouse for a new house built beside the track. *(W. E. Hayward).*

Although now extended to make a comfortable bungalow, Roadwater station still unmistakably shows its original purpose, making an interesting comparison with the photograph on page 44

When this photograph was taken about 1935, Roadwater crossing gates were still in position and the station house to the north was unaltered and used as a garden store. Today the southern gates have been removed and the old track converted into a public road. *(W. E. Hayward).*

Comberow station house as it was in 1933. Soon afterwards it was demolished for its stone and today only traces of the platform survive. *(T. R. Perkins. LGRP collection).*

Behind the station master's house the road to Comberow farm tunnels under the 1 in 4 gradient through this massive stone arch. The style is not unlike some of the mine buildings, the Mines Captain, Morgan Morgans, having acted as engineer for the completion of the incline.

Only a line of trees now picks out the incline as it ascends the 1 in 4 gradient beside the station master's house, although the viewpoint is the same as in the cover photograph. Since this view was taken about 1938 the higher woods have been felled and replanted with conifers, and it is no easier today to realise the towering majesty of the old incline. (R. Kingsley Tayler).

A modern guide book, commenting on the solidity of the engine house remains, remarks that 'the windows have steel frames, which is surprising to many of us who had the idea they were a twentieth century invention'. This photograph shows all that remained of the engine house in 1938, before Mr. V. C. Norman started rebuilding, intending to convert it to farm use. *(W. E. Hayward)*.

Today the rebuilt walls of the engine house have restored the outline of the huge embankment at the top of the incline. On the left are the old Stores, now a farmhouse, and although Railway Arch was demolished in 1923 it is still possible to recognise the scene as that shown in the 1905 photograph on page 32.

Only a grassy slope marks the track of the incline and Comberow is hidden in the trees 800 feet below, but from the summit the lower line can just be seen where it runs north eastwards past Timwood, before curving west through Pit Wood below Nettlecombe Clump.

In contrast to the preceding photograph, the view to the south from the top of the incline is across the level tableland on the ridge of the Brendons. Though taken almost fifty-five years after the illustration on page 32, the Stores and the station house can still clearly be seen in this 1959 picture from above the engine house ruins.

There are ducks in the old quarry, but the landmarks in the 1911 photograph on page 33 are still recognisable in this view forty-eight years later. The station is now a bungalow and the Stores a farmhouse, but even the wind driven electric generator could be mistaken for a signal as it stands on the line apparently guarding the incline.

Solid rather than handsome, Sea View House was the residence of the Mines Captain and stands within sight of the incline completed under the supervision of its most famous occupant, Morgan Morgans. *(H. H. Hole).*

Though most of the mining village of Brendon Hill has gone, Beulah Chapel today is a pleasant contrast to the forlorn picture on page 34. Restored in 1910 under the leadership of the circuit minister, the Rev. T. G. Jacob, the former Bible Christian chapel now serves a widely scattered Methodist congregation, as well as having been a regular meeting place for August Bank Holiday circuit rallies.

After the mines had closed the Raleigh's Cross Inn was described as 'a large, but now rather desolate, hostelry', but it was modernised by Mr. and Mrs. Preece when they moved here from the Egremont at Williton in 1937 and combined hotel keeping with farming. Today it provides a comfortable stop for refreshment when exploring the railway and mines, though rather different in appearance from the earlier photograph on page 34.

Burrow Farm engine house, the sole survivor on the Brendons since the demolition of the one at Kennesome Hill mine in 1978. Of typical Cornish style it was probably built about 1880 to the design of Captain Henry Skewis, the Cornish Mines Captain, and housed a 25-inch combined pumping and winding beam engine.

The broken trackbed is still plainly apparent in this view looking west from Withiel Hill towards the site of Luxborough Road station. Behind the second cottage (known from its shape as the Round House) was one of the earliest mines at Lothbrook, while Kennesome Hill engine house is hidden in the distant conifer forest.

Gupworthy Chapel was converted from two single storey miners' cottages, there being originally two terraces of cottages facing the mine, known grandly as The Square. Services were held here until 1972 when the tenancy (at £1 per year) was given up and the building subsequently sold to be incorporated into a bungalow.

Though this photograph of Gupworthy terminus was taken more than fifty years later than the illustration on page 36, the station house is little altered. On the left the stone goods shed and weighbridge house still stand, and by the loading dock a few upright timbers remain to show that they once formed part of the wooden store.

In the winter drifting snow would often block the cuttings on the upper section, and the 'Box' engine would be used as a battering ram to try and force its way through. This photograph of Gupworthy from the buffer stops was taken in 1962, but it would not be difficult to imagine that rusting rails still lay beneath the snow – so little has it changed.